Unlocking The Evidence

The new disability business case

First published in 2001 by
The Employers, Forum on Disability
Nutmeg House
60 Gainsford Street
London SE1 2NY
Tel: 0207 403 3020
Fax: 0207 403 0404
Web: www.employers-forum.co.uk

© Employers' Forum on Disability
ISBN 1 903894 01-8

This publication is protected by copyright law. If you make unauthorised copies from these pages, the publisher could take you and your employer to court and claim legal damages. Apart from any fair dealing for the purposes of review, as permitted under the Copyright, Designs and Patents Act 1988, this publication may only be reproduced, stored or transmitted, in any form, or by any means, with the prior permission in writing of the publishers.

Designed by: Jewell Design, Hove
Printed by: Hubbard Print, Sheffield

This publication is available in other formats

Unlocking The Evidence

The new disability business case

by
Simon Zadek
and
Susan Scott-Parker

employers'
forum on
disability

Sponsored by
BT

employers'
forum on
disability

THE GOLD CARD GROUP
• Abbey National • BBC • Barclays • BG • BT • BUPA •
• Camelot Group • Cable & Wireless • Centrica •
• Goldman Sachs • GlaxoSmithKline • Granada Group •
• HSBC • Inland Revenue • Kingfisher • Manpower •
• McDonald's Restaurants • Post Office • Railtrack •
• Sainsbury's Supermarkets • ScottishPower • Unum •

Unlocking The Evidence

Contents

1. Introduction	9
2. The Challenge	13
3. Transcending Compliance	19
4. Working Towards Mutual Benefit	23
5. Personal Performance	25
6. Accessing the 'Disabled Market'	33
7. The Virtuous Circle	45
8. The Strategic Business Case	51
9. So Why Are People Unconvinced?	55
10. Building Tomorrow's Sustainable Business	63
11. Diversity Futures?	71
12. Recommendations and Commitments	81
13. Conclusion	87
References	89
Author Biographies	97

"People have impairments – disability is what we do to them."

Simon Zadek

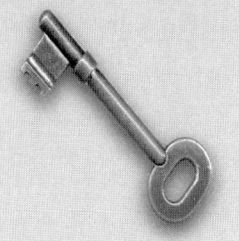

Introduction   1

Managing a diverse workforce is increasingly recognised as a key factor in improving efficiency, productivity and overall business success. Globalisation has accelerated and reinforced the need to embrace diversity. A highly significant element of the diversity debate – often overlooked – is disability. There are over 8.7 million disabled people in the UK alone, making up a large and growing proportion of employees, existing and potential customers, stakeholders and indeed shareholders.

However, by the year 2004, 40 per cent of the UK population will be over 45 – the age at which the incidence of disability begins to increase significantly. Disability, as part of the growth of diversity, is moving from an ethical responsibility to a business imperative.

The business case for employing disabled people is compelling. The individual performances and contribution far outweigh the relatively inexpensive (and often government funded) adjustments which may be necessary. Knowledge of the needs and expectations of a growing sector of the market combined with enhanced morale and people management systems are tangible benefits for companies who are good employers of disabled people.

A small number of leading companies have demonstrated these business benefits. However, many other businesses have yet to realise the rewards. Poor presentation of the business case is one reason why business people remain unconvinced, but more significantly, the exclusion of disabled people is rooted in fear and stereotyping. 'Unlocking The Evidence' presents arguments that go beyond simple cost benefit analysis. It offers a long term strategic case integrated into, and consistent with, the broader diversity perspective; a case that is sufficiently powerful to challenge the deep-rooted assumptions which currently prevent potential business benefits from being realised.

Exclusion from the workplace has a negative impact on individuals; places a financial cost on society; a taxation burden on businesses and hence affects profitability and competitiveness. Disability, therefore, is clearly a strategic issue, risk and opportunity for every business.

Tomorrow's most successful companies will be those which enable everyone to channel their skills, experience and energies towards business success; which recognise and welcome a diverse customer and stakeholder base, and thereby appeal to the increasingly discerning investor. Tomorrow's most successful societies will be those that most effectively meet the dual challenges of social cohesion and economic competitiveness.

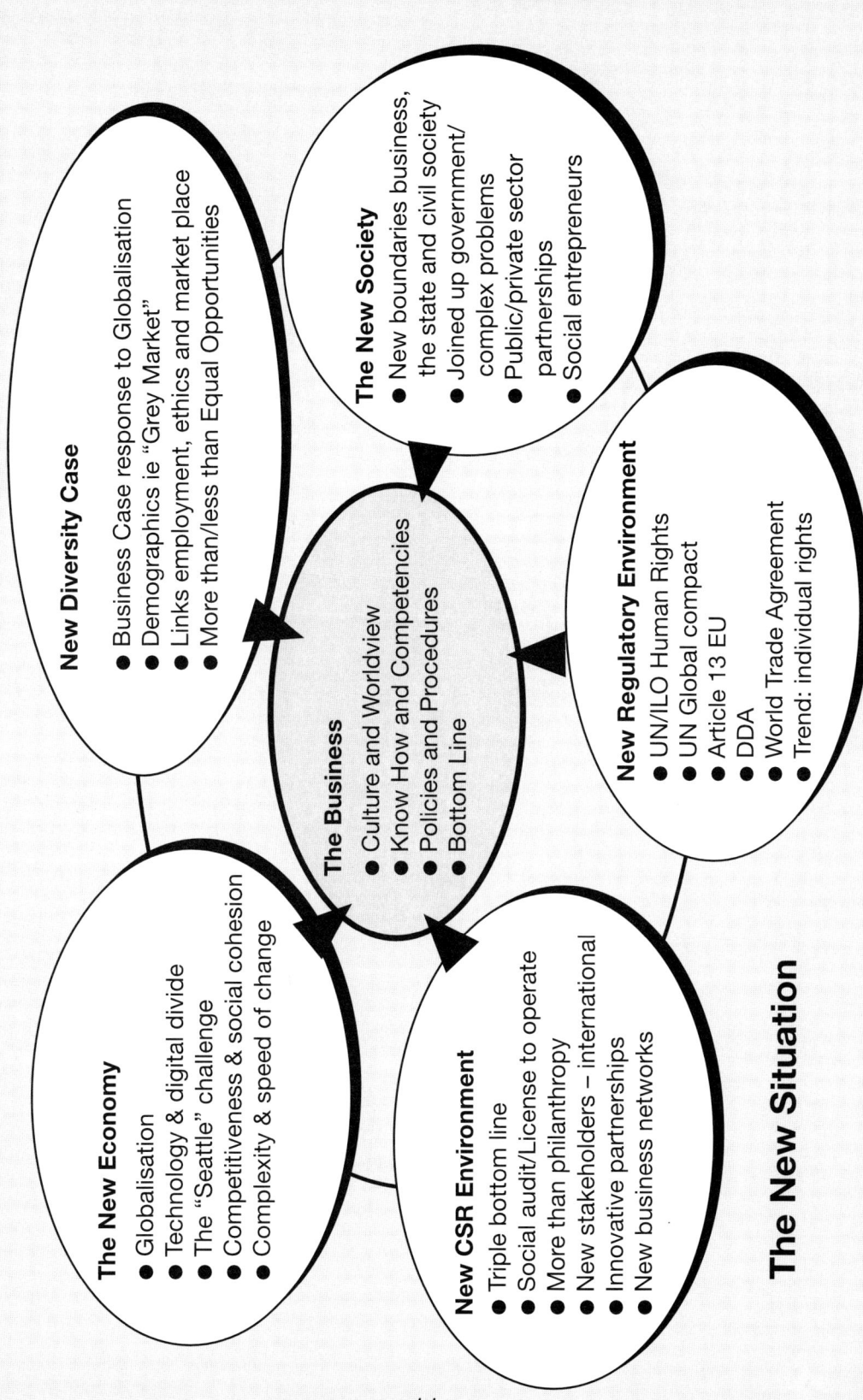

The Challenge 2

The challenge is to overcome a disabling environment so that everyone can contribute to, and gain from, organisations that base their competitive advantage on an inclusive approach. Unfortunately the standard set of statistics and arguments which comprise the business case, designed to influence employers to recruit and retain disabled people on merit, is not persuasive.

Discrimination against disabled people, based on assumptions regarding their potential, continues to restrict their work opportunities and their ability to contribute their energies, skills, and creativity in strengthening business and enriching society as a whole.

SOME FACTS ABOUT DISABILITY

- there are 8.7 million disabled people in the UK[1]
- **3 per cent of disabled people are born with a disability**
- 33 per cent of people over 55 have a disability
- **5.1 million people with disabilities are of working age**
- only 4 per cent of disabled people of working age require additional aids in the workplace or need health related treatment that would interfere with their work
- **unemployed disabled people are five times less likely to move into work than non-disabled counterparts[2]**
- there are 2.4 million disabled people out of work on benefits; around a million are actively seeking work
- **58 per cent of disabled people in work earn less than £10,000 per annum compared to a national average of 30 per cent**

Source: Department for Education and Employment

Most disabled people are not disabled at birth. About 77 per cent of disabled people became disabled after the age of 16, i.e. once they were of working age. Of this group, the vast majority, over 97 per cent, had been in paid work at some time before they become disabled[3]. Many impairments correlate with age - particularly those associated with restricted locomotion, reaching, stretching, and dexterity, as well as hearing and vision[4]. 30 per cent of those aged 50-59 years are disabled, compared with only 10 per cent for the 20-29 age group.

By 2036, over 15 million people in the UK will be over 65, a more than 30 per cent increase over current levels. As our society 'greys', the percentage of people with disabilities will go up. One study predicts an estimated increase in the numbers of people with disabilities of 23 per cent between 1995 and 2020, an increase primarily associated with the ageing population[5].

These statistics illustrate the results of historic patterns of discrimination. They describe today's situation despite legislation such as the Disability Discrimination Act (1995), and despite an extensive network of individuals, groups and organisations committed to promoting the interests of disabled people.

The fact that people with disabilities continue to be excluded from work is damaging and costly to society at large, as well as directly to the individuals and their families.

THE ECONOMIC COST

- there is an unquantified but enormous loss to society of the productive capacities of disabled people who cannot find employment or, for those in work, whose potential is not fully utilised
- **59 per cent of disabled people live in a 'family' where no-one is in paid work**[6]
- most people become disabled well into their adult, working lives, often when in employment. Employers face the costs associated with the loss of trained and experienced employees moving prematurely onto benefits and pensions. Studies in the USA, for example, indicate an average return of US$30 on every $1 spent accommodating people who become disabled, as one element of a 'skill retention strategy'[7]. The UK Post Office estimates each early retirement on health grounds costs up to £80,000
- **annual UK expenditure on benefits to disabled people has grown by 3.5% per annum throughout the 1990s' to £24.3 billion in 1998/99**[8]**. This is expected to grow by a further £1.7 billion by 2001/2**[9]
- these costs are a charge to the UK's economy, negatively affecting its competitiveness. 3000 people each week move into Incapacity Benefit: only 10% will ever move back into work[10]

Disabled People in Great Britain of Working Age by Impairment and Employment Status

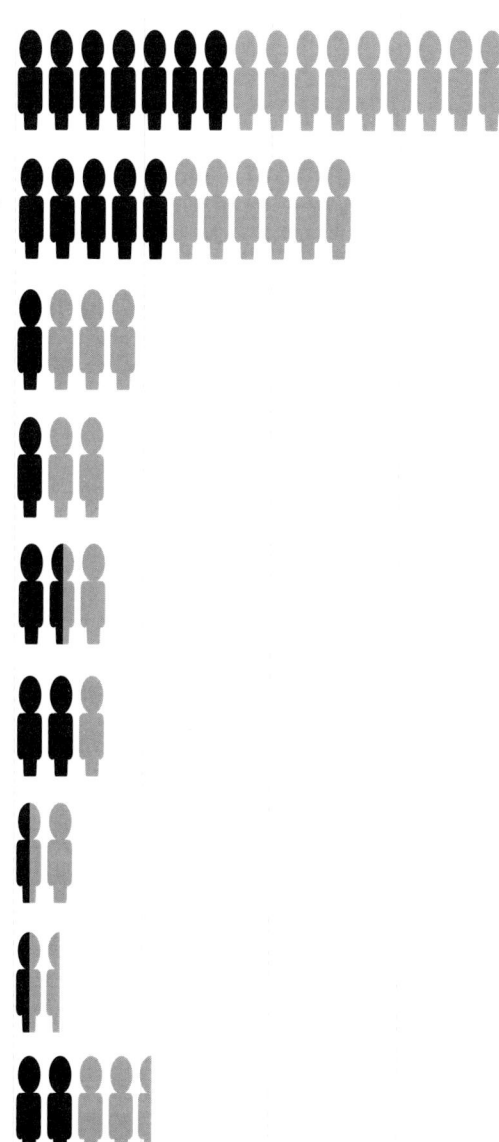

musculoskeletal
e.g. problems with arms, hands, legs feet back and neck

chest, breathing problems, heart, blood pressure

mental health problems

stomach, liver, kidney, digestion

sensory (vision and hearing)

diabetes

progressive conditions
eg. Parkinson's disease, arthritis and MS

learning difficulties

other disabilities
including epilepsy, skin conditions and speech impediments

■ in employment
▨ not in employment

disabled people of working age (%)

Source: DfEE Disability Briefing: November 2000

These costs of exclusion are, however, only part of the story. They do not reflect the loss of competitiveness associated with the failure of business to take advantage of the potential contribution of disabled people.

Such disadvantage is comparable in many ways to that resulting from sexism, racism, ageism and other forms of discrimination. The call for 'equal opportunities' for disabled people and for anti-discrimination legislation arises from a rejection of injustice; at the same time, equal opportunities and the related principle of 'diversity' are increasingly seen as a core factor in determining business efficiency, productivity, and broader economic success.

The challenge is formidable. The cost of continued exclusion of disabled people from the UK and global economy is enormous and growing. Everyone - business, disabled people, society - gains by creating an environment that actively enables everyone, including disabled people, to engage in creative and rewarding work.

Transcending Compliance 3

Legislative changes alone cannot deliver an enabling environment for people with impairments. Historically the business case has been argued principally in terms of legal compliance and corporate philanthropy. The legal argument has become more high profile in the UK since the Disability Discrimination Act came into force in 1995. Since then it has been unlawful to discriminate against a 'disabled person' in terms of either their access to employment or to goods, services, and facilities. However, businesses which employ fewer than 15 people are currently exempt from the employment provisions. Discrimination by these small organisations is technically 'acceptable' in law - although the government is committed to removing the exclusion. The Act protects everyone considered disabled in that they have a physical or mental impairment that has a substantial and long-term adverse effect on a person's ability to carry out normal day to day activities[11].

There are estimated to be over 8.7 million people in the UK who fall under the Act, plus an additional 1.3 million who are protected because they were disabled in the past.

Some Countries with Disability Discrimination Legislation

AUSTRALIA
Disability Discrimination Act (1992)

CANADA
Employment Equity Act/
Canadian Human Rights Act

FRANCE
Disability Act (1975)

IRELAND
Employment Equality Act (1998)

PORTUGAL
Comprehensive law of 1989 (no. 9/89)

NEW ZEALAND
Human Rights Act 1993.

SOUTH AFRICA
Employment Equity Act (1998)

UNITED KINGDOM
Disability Discrimination Act (1995)

UNITED STATES OF AMERICA
Americans with Disabilities Act (1990)

HONG KONG
Disability Discrimination Ordinance (1995)

Legislation to further the inclusion of disabled people has become a global phenomenon reinforcing a very different way of thinking about and defining disability. Global business will need to understand and respond.

It is too early to say how effective disability discrimination legislation will be in improving the day-to-day experience of disabled people seeking work. However, the US-based National Organization on Disability has recently published a survey that aimed to assess the early effects of the Americans with Disabilities Act 1990[12]. The survey, while controversial, provides food for thought. It suggests, for example, that the proportion of disabled people in employment has actually declined in the US since 1986. It also found that fewer than four out of ten disabled people say that their job requires their full talents and abilities. Finally, and perhaps most worrying is that they conclude that there has been a slight increase since 1994 in the proportion of disabled people saying that they experience job discrimination.

It is always difficult to assess the impact of anti-discrimination legislation. For example, in contrast to the National Organization on Disability findings is another American source that claims 800,000 people with severe disabilities have found work since the ADA came into force[13]. What is increasingly agreed is that legislation, whilst critically important, cannot alone remove discrimination against disabled people in the labour market.

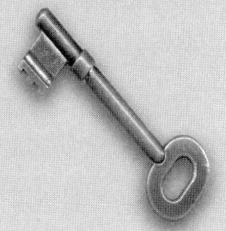

Working Towards Mutual Benefit 4

Recognising the potential for mutual benefit is the key if more disabled people are to work in the heart of tomorrow's companies. The core message is that employing disabled people can enhance business profitability.

The leading edge of thinking and practice is steadily shifting beyond compliance and well-meaning philanthropy, towards a solutions-focused culture which shifts the emphasis from the person's disability to what can be done which will enable that person to contribute.

This culture change recognises that disabled people can and do add business benefits over and above the avoidance of censure or legal penalties.

FACTS

THE PRINCIPAL BUSINESS BENEFITS CAN BE GROUPED AS FOLLOWS:

- the personal performance of disabled people using traditional measures of efficiency and productivity

- the general performance of the company which recruits, retains and develops disabled employees, particularly through:

    – better people management systems.

    – the long-term business impact of reputational gains

    – the positive impact of employing disabled people on the morale and motivation of other employees

- the ability of disabled employees to help companies access the significant market of disabled consumers, their families and friends

Personal Performance 5

The received wisdom that disabled people 'must of course' be significantly less productive than their non-disabled colleagues is the bedrock on which the exclusion of disabled people is rationalised. Given the significance of this assumption, there is a surprising lack of research examining the workplace productivity of disabled people as compared to their non-disabled counterparts. More significant, perhaps, is the lack of awareness that the research which has been done flatly contradicts this received wisdom.

Research commissioned by the UK government's Employment Department in the late 1980s throws some light on the matter of performance[14]. Based on a survey of business managers, 82 per cent of respondents concluded that the attendance record of disabled people was the same or better than other employees. More significantly, 79 per cent of respondents stated that, in their direct experience, disabled people performed the same or better than other employees.

Company-based surveys consistently conclude that the experience of working with disabled people results in a growing demand to increase the number of disabled people in the workplace. Actual exposure to working with disabled people has a positive reinforcement effect.

Performance is always a balance of costs and contribution. While most disabled people do not require adjustments at work, the costs involved in creating a suitable work environment for a disabled person can usually be managed alongside other flexible work practices. These costs are generally not significant, and can often be offset through assistance through various government programmes. 'Marks and Spencer have documented that two thirds of the adjustments they make for people with disabilities cost nothing'[15].

A study by the National Institute of Disability Management and Research in Canada concluded that 'co-ordinated work-based disability management has a significant impact on reducing costs associated with workplace injury and disability'. In their own words, 'workplace-based disability case management is a return-to-work process for workers with disabilities using services, people and materials designed to minimise the impact and economic/human cost of disability to workers, employers and society at large. The process is workplace-based, managed and directed in consultation and co-operation with all relevant parties'[16].

Similarly, company based studies such as that undertaken by British Colombia Hydro and Power Authority in Canada confirm that companies which actively engage in accommodating people with disabilities see reductions in overall workplace injury and sickness absenteeism, with associated cost savings.

PEOPLE AND PERFORMANCE:
Centrica

Centrica, a major supplier of energy and services to homes and businesses in Great Britain, recruited 50 disabled people as part of a Welfare to Work project in Manchester. Centrica plans to continue to employ people with disabilities because they have seen the following benefits:

- **motivated and high performing staff**

- reduced staff turnover

- **a more diverse workforce which better reflects customer base**

- raised awareness of issues affecting disabled people, carers and the long term unemployed

- **managers' are more skilled in recruiting and managing a diverse workforce**

- enhanced corporate reputation

Source:
Richard Bide, Group Director of Human Resources, Centrica plc.

COMPANY PERFORMANCE: DuPont

The best known company-based study to explore the productivity of disabled people is DuPont[17]. The most recent element of this 20-year tracking study was published in 1990 and covered 811 disabled employees. Of these, almost 70per cent acquired disabilities whilst with DuPont. Almost 20 per cent were management and professional employees. The study concludes that:

'For 35 years, surveys have consistently shown that DuPont employees with disabilities, equal or exceed their co-workers without disabilities in terms of job performance, attendance, and safety commitment'.

NEW MARKET: Tricon Restaurants Australia Pty Limited

CASE STUDY

While Tricon Restaurants Australia Pty Limited has a 'long and proud commitment' to the recruitment of employees with disabilities, they felt their efforts were hampered by management concerns about productivity, costs and recruitment/training complexity. Tricon established the Jobsplus Program in early 1994 and specifically set out to measure the results:

A summary of results follows:

- 180 employees with disabilities were recruited between March 1994 and February 1996

- **94 per cent of employees were recruited through a disability employment agency or rehabilitation service at no cost to the company**

- Jobsplus employees had retention rates 4.5 times higher than other employees

- **Jobsplus employees achieved 100 per cent on job safety, i.e. nil accidents during the two year period**

- 48 per cent of Jobsplus employees attracted a government wage subsidy or funded work experience for the on-the-job training period

- **restaurant managers rated 85 per cent of Jobsplus employees as equal to or better than average for on the job performance**

- **restaurant managers rated 92 per cent of Jobsplus employees equal to or better than average on work attitude**

- **59 per cent of restaurant managers rated the service provided by disability employment agency to be very good or excellent**

- 66 per cent of Jobsplus employees rated the support of the restaurant manager to be very good or excellent

- **97 per cent of Jobsplus employees stated that co-workers were friendly and 97 per cent stated that they felt like part of the restaurant team**

This study was a key catalyst for Tricon continuing and extending the Jobsplus Program.

MANAGING ABSENCE: Barclays

Barclays' job applicants used to receive a medical examination if:

- applying for management positions
- **disabled**
- they did not complete the Health Declaration on the Bank's application form or if their answers prompted further questions about their medical history

In November 1993, Barclays reviewed total sickness absence over the previous two years for a random sample of 200 disabled and 200 non-disabled staff. This included typical levels and reasons for absence. The non-disabled sample included both those who had and had not received a pre-employment medical. The survey showed:

- disabled staff on average had eight days absence over the period
- **non-disabled staff had on average ten days absence over the period.**

The Bank was unable to find any correlation between the disclosure on the Health Declaration and subsequent sickness absence, and it was considered unnecessary to continue giving medicals to such large numbers of job applicants. During 1995 far fewer medicals were undertaken with no adverse impact on absenteeism levels.

DISABILITY MANAGEMENT PROGRAMME

British Columbia Hydro and Power Authority[18]:

BC Hydro is the third largest electrical utility in Canada. Employee absences through sick leave, long term disability and workers' compensation-related injury (WCB) were costing BC Hydro approximately $15 million per year. It became clear that disability-related costs could be significantly lowered by reducing the frequency and duration of injury and disability.

The company needed to be more expert in making adjustments for disabled workers and enhance their understanding of disability as it affected their organisation.

Although the BC Hydro programme is relatively new, significant trends and cost savings are evident.

- **reducing the frequency and duration of absences due to illness and disability was a primary goal. Data shows that lost time has decreased by 65 per cent**

- the programme is projected to realise a saving of over $1 million over the next 4 years

Accessing the 'Disabled Market' 6

Disabled people can make distinct and positive contributions to business success by virtue of their experience of being disabled; the knowledge this gives them of the needs of other disabled stakeholders, notably customers and through the increased morale and productivity of non-disabled work colleagues.

There is a growing recognition by business of the significance of the 'disabled market', particularly in the retail, financial, e-commerce and tourism sectors. The importance of the 'disability pound' increasingly holds true for designers, manufacturers, and suppliers of consumer products and related industries, such as advertising and communications.

Given the heterogeneity of the disabled 'community', the size of the market is difficult to estimate. However, analysis of research by the Institute of Employment Studies gives a figure of £45-50 billion per annum, or about 10 per cent of the UK's total annual domestic consumption[19]. This market will grow as the population 'greys'.

The 'grey market' in the UK is both an exciting marketing opportunity and a daunting social challenge. It is particularly significant that many older consumers welcome more accessible products and services even if they have yet to describe (or may never describe) their visual or hearing or mobility impairment as a disability.

Key Note, a leading UK market research company, defines 'greys' as those aged 45 and above - already 47.4 per cent of the UK's total adult population. Over the next 30 years, their numbers will expand dramatically and by the year 2031, 60.4 per cent of adults will be over 45 years of age[20].

GREY SPENDING POWER IN THE UK

The annual income of the over-50s currently exceeds £160 billion; they have an 85 per cent share of the UK's private wealth.

Over-55s are:

- 48 per cent more likely than average to spend their day spending in the shops and 14 per cent more likely to eat out

- **likely to spend over a third more on their cars than average buyers**

- 80 per cent more likely than a typical person to buy a brand new car

- **35 per cent more likely to go on a foreign holiday and spend over two-thirds more than average per holiday**

- 80 per cent more likely to invest in shares and almost two-thirds more likely to have a gold card

Source:
Mike Freeney, Disability Matters Limited[21]

This demographic revolution will shift the epicentre of consumer activity from the current exclusive focus on youth to matching the needs, challenges and aspirations of middle-aged and mature consumers. Companies whose products and services are aligned with the age-related and disability-related needs of new generations of maturing customers are on the threshold of tremendous opportunity.

Effectively accessing this large and growing market requires relevant information, know-how and skills. The Institute of Employment Studies, in a recent report, concluded that most businesses are aware of the fact of the disabled market, and furthermore consider themselves to be aware as to how to effectively service this market[22]. However, the same study concludes that business has a restricted view of disability - usually limited to visible mobility impairments. In fact, fewer than 5 per cent of disabled people in the UK are wheelchair users. The figure is significant because:

● the relatively few wheelchair users encountered on a daily basis, reinforces the assumption that the numbers of people significantly affected by disability is very small

● access for their presumed wheelchairs is assumed to be too expensive and too difficult

The 'Left Out' report, published by UK charity Scope, surveyed more than 500 businesses and found that almost three in four presented problems for disabled people. Deloitte Touche, in 1993, pointed out that the tourist market alone had an estimated earning potential of £23.4 billion[23].

Another survey of FTSE 100 and FTSE 250 companies found that almost a third of participants were not aware that they need to change the way they provide services to the public to comply with the Disability Discrimination Act. The survey, conducted in April 2000, highlighted the uncertainty amongst some of the largest organisations in the country about the implications of the DDA and also the business potential[24].

Consumer Expenditure

In the USA, the President's Committee on Employment of People with Disabilities estimated that the annual discretionary spending of disabled people was US$175 billion (£109 billion). This figure is almost three times as much as the USA teenage discretionary spend, so actively courted by business.

Source: President's Committee on Employment of People with Disabilities 1998

Tourism in Europe

'Now, with this study, the size and spending power of the potential market across Europe is demonstrated. With good transport, accessible facilities and properly trained staff the gates will open not just to the 5 million disabled people who are currently able to travel, but to 19 million; not just to the current 3 per cent of all tourists but to 10 per cent; not merely to the £6,500 million that is currently spent, but to £23,400 million.'

Tourism 2000 - Tourism for all in Europe, Report by Deloitte Touche , 1993

A Positive Attitude

In the USA, McDonalds ran a TV advertising campaign featuring people with hearing impairments who are seen signing each other about where to go for a meal. When they ask for a meal in McDonalds the assistant signs back 'is that with regular or large fries'. As a result of the campaign, McDonalds became a favourite restaurant for hearing impaired people in the USA.

> **"Our biggest conference, worth £350,000, came to us because we were accessible"**
>
> Robert Peel, Chief Executive,
> Mount Charlotte Thistle Hotels

Genuine access is a broader and more powerful concept than the usual narrow focus on wheelchair access. The results of a recent survey of UK retail staff 'real situation' responses to customers with disabilities[25] concluded that:

- 54 per cent of the disabled customers felt that the staff serving them had not received relevant disability training

- **83 per cent of companies were unable to provide specific information in an alternative format, i.e. large print**

- 74 per cent of the deaf or hard of hearing customers did not see a sign indicating the provision of a loop system at the customer service desk

- **61 per cent of loop systems tested by the deaf or hard of hearing were found not to be working properly**

- 72 per cent of the buildings visited did not have any public information symbols displayed on the outside indicating what provisions were available to their disabled customers

- **40 per cent of wheelchair users had difficulties entering the buildings**

- 44 per cent of disabled customers found counters at the cash points or customer service desks an unsuitable height

Source: The Challenge of Disability, Research Report 1 – November 1998, Grass Roots Group Plc

Technology Talks

Understanding the needs of disabled people requires dialogue with disabled people themselves. In the UK, BT, for example, places considerable store on their 'Age and Disability Committee' set up to assess the needs of these two enormous customer and staff groups, and to help BT to mould services and products to meet these needs. Through this process, BT has evolved Typetalk to ensure access for disabled people who would previously have been excluded from a key growth area of communication services.

'Typetalk' was established by BT to enable customers with hearing or speech difficulties to be independent of friends or family in making use of telephone services. It involves over 600 operators who can support up to 50,000 text users making half a million calls a month[26].

The accelerating use and availability of the Internet as a medium in which to conduct business and purchase goods and services represents a significant opportunity. The internet is increasingly attractive for many disabled people as it removes the obvious barriers of location and distance. It also removes unintentional prejudice given that transactions are electronic and impersonal and do not require the person to deal with the vendor or service provider face-to-face. However, much of the potential economic purchasing power of disabled people will be lost to businesses if their on line services are so poorly designed that a significant sector of society is unable to use them.

The new economy will also create the demand for business to business transactions to address the disability dimension. Thus any organisation which commissions new IT systems will expect the supplier to ensure the new system is accessible to disabled employees, customers and other stakeholders.

Employees Feedback

There is clearly a role for disabled and older employees to raise awareness in their organisations regarding the potential of the disabled market. This link between market opportunities and employment is made starkly clear by Littlewoods amongst others; 'To succeed in a fiercely-competitive economic climate an organisation needs to get closer to its customers. A diverse workforce is a potential source of accurate and unbiased information about existing and potential customers, and can help a company plan more successful marketing or service delivery strategies'[27].

Employee – Customer Virtuous Circle: B&Q

B&Q has achieved a major breakthrough in recognising the value of employing older and disabled people in their stores as business results demonstrate they are more attuned to the needs of their customers. "The vision for B&Q is that we want disabled people to be able to shop with confidence in our stores secure in the knowledge that they will be able to access our goods and services easily, find solutions to meet their needs and be treated with respect by our store staff".

In doing this, B&Q achieves the following:

- increased sales to disabled people

- **brand enhancement linked to 'good neighbour' policy and practice**

- overall improvement in customer care on the principle that 'if we get it right for disabled people, then we get it right for most people'

- **increased overall employee satisfaction, and therefore better retention, absenteeism, and productivity rates**

Source: Kay Allen, Equal Opportunities and Diversity Manager, B&Q, July 2000

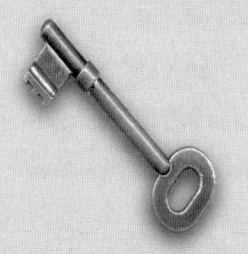

The Virtuous Circle

The dynamic relationship between employing disabled people and the disability market is more complex and rewarding than it might first appear. Providing greater access to disabled customers changes their overall perception of the company, as well as the perception of their families, carers, and friends. B&Q has found that creating an attractive environment for both older and disabled customers has led to an increase in job applications from both groups; B&Q then is seen to employ disabled people, which in turn strengthens its position with customers and the community.

The B&Q Experience

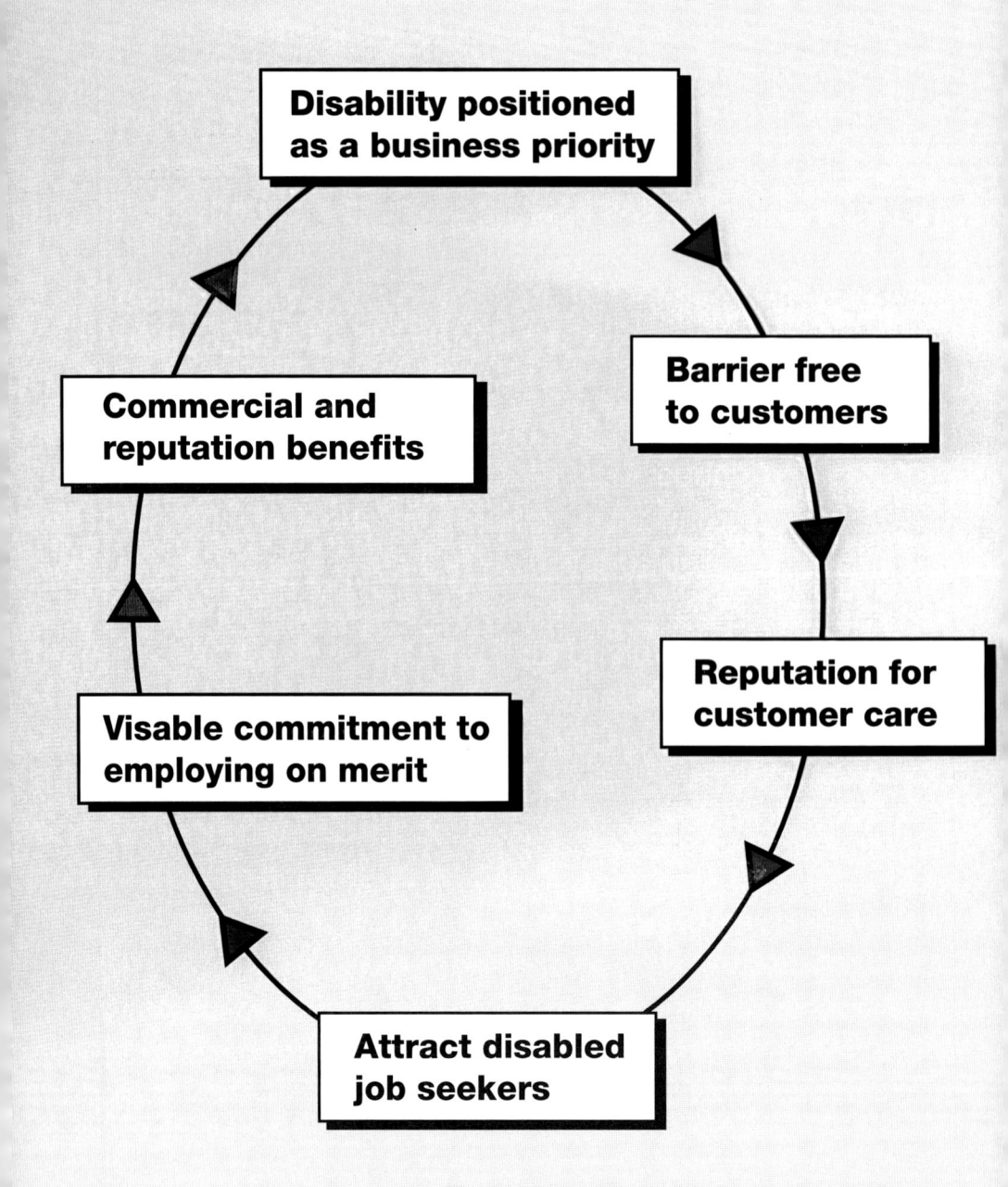

- Disability positioned as a business priority
- Barrier free to customers
- Reputation for customer care
- Attract disabled job seekers
- Visable commitment to employing on merit
- Commercial and reputation benefits

Effective people management contributes significantly to sustainable profitability. A recent 10-year study into business success concluded that people management practices and job design accounted for as much as 17 per cent of measured variations in productivity and profitability[28]. A recent analysis of more than 100 German companies revealed a strong link between investing in employees and stock market performance[29]. In the UK, the organisation promoting the main employee relations 'quality assurance' system, Investors in People, has argued that those companies adopting IIP out-perform the national average on a range of financial measures[30].

Links have also been drawn between satisfied employees and customer retention. Research by the UK public survey company, MORI, suggested that whereas 41% of those satisfied with their jobs will recommend their employer's products or services without being asked, this declines to just 4% of those dissatisfied with their jobs. Indeed, one third of those who are dissatisfied with their jobs will actually speak unfavourably about their employer's products or services without being asked[31].

Further research has shown how employee satisfaction is often correlated with customer satisfaction. When the two were correlated for bank branches, those which achieved high levels of employee satisfaction experienced, on average, 15 per cent higher customer satisfaction than other branches[32].

Good 'people management' includes a range of practices, from the quality of management to valuing individual contributions, to the quality of the work environment, to work-life balance policies and will invariably incorporate a significant disability dimension. There are good reasons for concluding a linkage between productivity, the employment of disabled people and the benefits of a diverse workforce:

- leading companies increasingly recognise the importance of a diverse workforce which mirrors the perspectives and needs of key stakeholders. Shell International, for example, has said that their miscalculation of the public's mood over the sinking of the Brent Spar oil platform might well have been avoided if senior management had been more diverse and hence more in touch with public opinion. Shell has therefore launched a drive with published targets to increase the diversity of their senior management team over the next decade

- one in four non-disabled people have a relation or a close friend who is disabled for whom they have some caring responsibilities. These people are likely to respond particularly well to those employers who are seen to ensure that disabled people have equal access to work and to products and services

- there is considerable anecdotal evidence that non-disabled employees feel empowered through gaining the understanding and expertise that allows them to work for, supervise, work alongside and/or serve disabled people more effectively

- employing disabled managers and staff signals to existing and potential staff that the company is a 'caring company' which treats people fairly (remembering that most disabled people become disabled while in work). This can in turn increase applications from, and retention of, good people and more generally improve morale and productivity[33]

- a company's openness to employing disabled people ensures improved access to a wider pool of talent

Fair Treatment and Employee Satisfaction

The 1998 Workplace Employee Relations Survey, the largest ever survey of employee attitudes in Britain, found that 'where employees thought that management showed understanding about balancing work and family responsibilities, encouraged skill development, involved them and treated them fairly, they are much more likely to be satisfied'.

**Source: Britain at Work,
Mark Cully et al, Routledge, 1999**

Diversity
the strategic benefits

Global business case
- accessing new markets
- product service development
- navigating complexity
- deepening organisational values
- benefiting from diversity

Societal
- reducing social costs
- improving productivity
- strengthening cohesion and innovation

Organisational
- cost benefit
- team morale
- quality people management systems

Personal
- recognition and growth
- overcoming fear and stigma
- new leadership
- work/family links

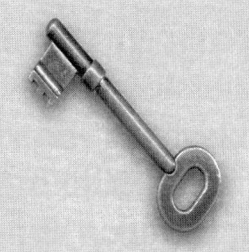

The Strategic Business Case   8

The core message of the new disability business case is that employing disabled people can enhance business profitability and unlock potential. Businesses that embrace disability as part of a diversity programme will be able to

- access untapped reserves of talent

- open up new markets

- improve operational efficiency: reduced costs, lower turnover, improved efficiency and service delivery, minimised litigation

- promote new sources of ideas, creativity and problem solving

- enhance reputation and loyalty both internally and from external stakeholders and customers

- build brand loyalty and distinctiveness by valuing all customers and employees as individuals

Globalisation accelerates the significance of diversity. It accentuates the need to define common values and to build business relationships that embrace increasing levels of diversity, in terms, for example, of location, culture, religion, language, age and ethnicity and disability. Globalisation also accelerates the need to address the disability dimension as a significant public policy priority.

Public Policy – Addressing the Disability dimension

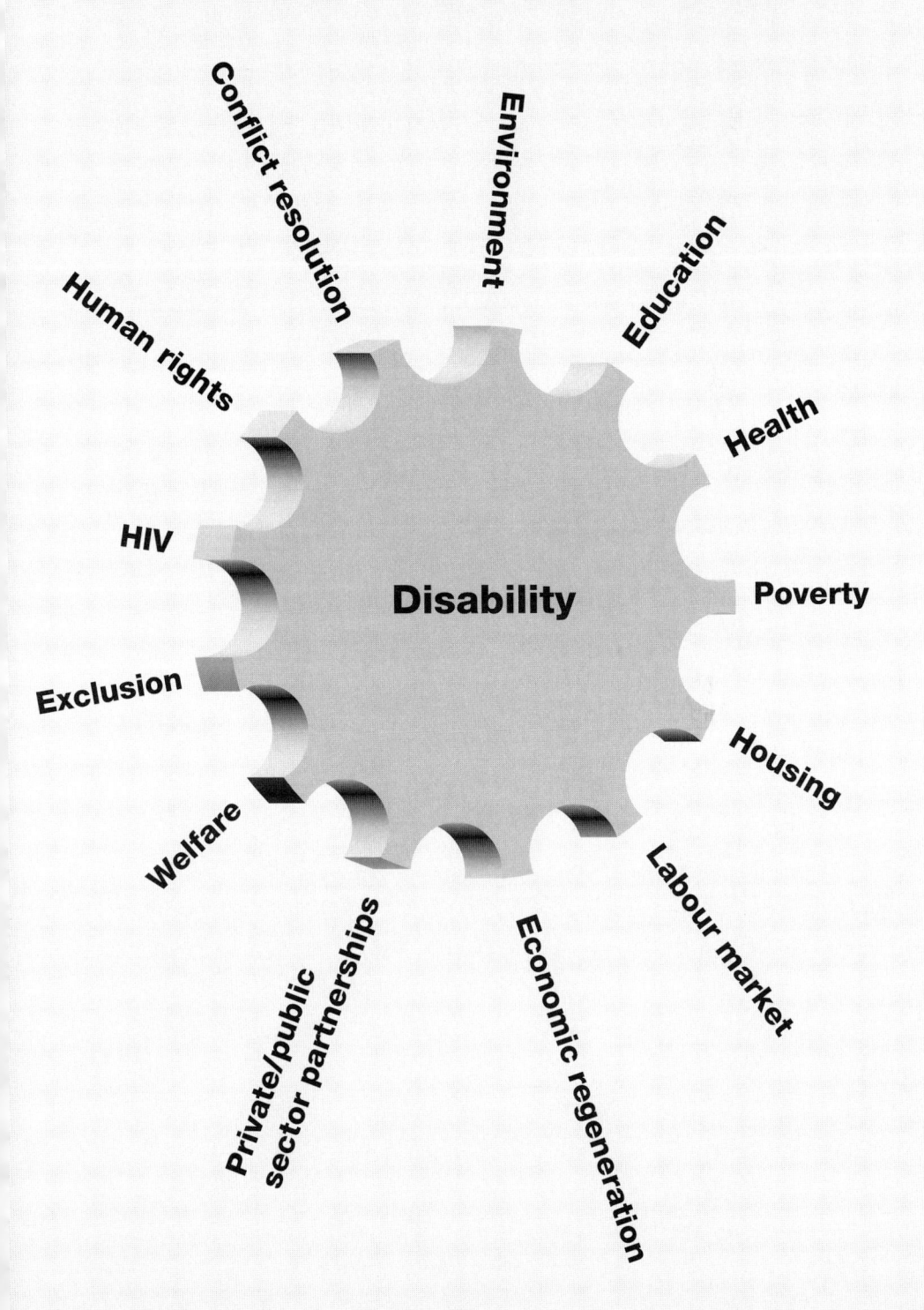

Disability

- Conflict resolution
- Environment
- Education
- Health
- Poverty
- Housing
- Labour market
- Economic regeneration
- Private/public sector partnerships
- Welfare
- Exclusion
- HIV
- Human rights

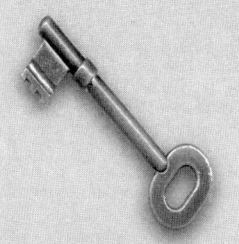

So Why Are People Unconvinced? 9

The exclusion of disabled people from the workplace cannot be understood simply through the calculus of 'economic cost-benefit'. For that matter, neither can successful long-term business strategies.

Why is it that so few organisations recruit, employ, and retain so few disabled people? Why does the 'robust' business case fail to convince so many senior managers and directors? Why is the evidence actively ignored by those who mould the cultures, values and attitudes of their organisations?

It is noteworthy that it is not only the private sector that fails to employ disabled people. The same is true of the public sector. While it is governments who legislate and empower the Commissions, they too find it difficult to practice what they preach.

The systematic exclusion of disabled people from the workplace must be understood in the wider context of barriers to achieving equal opportunities and diversity more generally. People reject diversity as a business priority for essentially the same reasons, whether one is addressing discrimination associated with physical, sensory or psychological impairments, or other avenues for social exclusion such as age, gender, sexual orientation, religion or ethnicity.

Specific and unique justifications for the exclusion of disabled people generally do, however, continue to be offered. These include, for example, objections that 'deaf people cannot communicate', that 'blind people cannot access information technology', or 'people with a history of mental health difficulty cannot cope in a fast moving environment'. It is objections like these - based on lack of information, lack of personal contact, false assumptions and fear - that any business case will need to counter if it is to change behaviour.

The fact that everyone can become disabled adds another unique and challenging dynamic.

It is in this context that one begins to understand why the business case – as usually presented – so often fails to convince or influence. This traditional presentation misses the point that the exclusion of disabled people is rooted in fear and stereotyping. Disabled people will continue to be regarded as the 'naturally' excluded so long as the lack of direct contact between business leaders and people with disabilities allows deeply-rooted fears and stereotypes to be perpetuated.

One view is that the disability 'business case' does not do the job because much of the evidence is weak and poorly articulated. It is true that the rationale for employing more disabled people is often poorly presented. There is a dearth of high quality material presenting information the business community regards as relevant, perhaps surprising given the sheer size of the disability support and lobbying community.

Furthermore, the few documents that are available start from a fundamentally flawed premise: that business people 'only respond to the numbers'. People in business do of course pay critical attention to the numbers, particularly those that directly bear on their financial bottom line. Yet, they also deeply distrust numbers which they cannot validate from their own direct, personal experience. Quantitative (and in this context often perceived to be cynical) statistical/financial predictions rarely empower someone to go against 'common sense and their better judgement'.

Indeed, reliance on statistics which attempt to describe disabled people in general terms, communicated so often by non-disabled advocates or 'experts', has reinforced the tendency to regard all people with disabilities as separate and similar, and thus may well hinder efforts by disabled people to be accepted as unique individuals.

A second argument is that the classic 'cost-benefit' business case simply misses the point. Rather than just being poorly communicated, it reflects the false assumption that people are persuaded to treat others with dignity and respect through the cost-benefit equations of accountants and economists.

A survey commissioned by The Post Office for the Employers' Forum on Disability concluded that line-managers rarely agreed with the view that the 'only thing that counts is what is counted'. The survey found that the most popular argument in favour of employing disabled people was the 'unquantifiable view' that it brought fresh ideas and perspectives to the table. Interestingly, these line managers also offered the unsolicited perspective that employing disabled people made sense because they had the same right to work as anyone else[34]. What comes across repeatedly in this context is that such attitudes are not 'unbusiness-like', but increasingly reflect the sorts of values that underpin best practice management and employee expectations.

As the Industrial Society concludes in a recent report:

'the new generation of business leaders [base their leadership] ... on mutual trust, shared beliefs, and strong relationships ... [they] ... recognise the leadership potential in everyone ... they have the values, the integrity, the enthusiasm, and the ability to gain trust'[35].

The sociology of exclusion is far more complex than any argument that merely distinguishes red from black ink at the bottom of the page. The emotional resistance to the inclusion of those percieved to be significantly different – "not like me" – is very powerful:

One typical survey of the attitudes of non-disabled towards disabled people found that:

- 58 per cent felt awkward and embarrassed in encountering disabled people

- 47 per cent felt fear during such encounters because they saw what might happen to them

- 25 per cent felt resentment or anger during such encounters[36]

Another survey shows that:

- 32 per cent of the UK public agreed there were people in society who assume a wheelchair user could not be intelligent[37]

Institutionalised and internalised, often inadvertent discrimination is not uncommon be it on the grounds of, for example, race, age, gender, religion or disability. Our knowledge of the deeply irrational prejudices and stereotypes that underpin discrimination should inform us all that genuine attitudinal change requires more than the 'cold logic' of statistics[38].

We cannot underestimate how difficult it is to overcome such deeply rooted resistance to accepting disabled people as individuals rather than as members of a stigmatised group. It is not a simple matter to communicate that disabled people are, after all, 'just people'. In this context, seemingly business-like statements such as 'we do not get qualified applicants' or 'we cannot carry passengers' or 'our first priority must be the business' or 'it would not be fair to expose disabled people to the pressure we all experience at work' must be treated with caution.

The traditional 'business case' fails because the link is not made between disability and the strategic needs of business. Disability is not usually presented in terms that are meaningful to the business community. This view is confirmed by, for example, any review of strategic management literature, and the main thrust of strategic management tools. Despite the 10,000 or so non-governmental organisations in the UK alone, committed to supporting disabled people, the issue is rarely on the strategic radar of business. Disability is still in the main deemed a 'social' rather than a business issue; as such, it would not require nor naturally acquire high-level business champions.

Business-to-business dialogue, routinely reinforced by personal contact with disabled people, supported by accurate information is usually far more effective.

A German Judge ruled in 1992 that a couple should be entitled to a reduction in the price of their holiday because disabled people were also at the hotel.

The Judge stated 'the unavoidable sight of the disabled person at close quarters during every meal caused nausea and was an incessant and unusually strong reminder of the possibilities of human suffering'.

The Judge went on to claim that 'the disabled are neither directly nor indirectly affected by this law suit'.
It was simply a matter of whether the holidaymaker or the company should have to 'bear the risk of . . . the unpleasant experience of meeting with the disabled'.

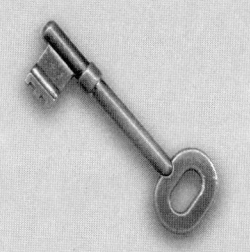

10
Building Tomorrow's Sustainable Business

The 'business case' for diversity and for intergrating disabled people into a diverse workforce is multidimensional and more persuasive than might first appear. The nuts and bolts of 'what things cost' and 'how business benefits' clearly count a great deal. But more is needed to deliver the underlying cultural changes that will permanently place disabled people and other disadvantaged groups on a level playing field of opportunity and reward.

For example, the drive towards 'corporate social responsibility' across a growing part of the corporate community is now often placed in the context of business gains. A recent study by The Conference Board of Europe concluded that, 'while positive effects of corporate citizenship may not be measurable, studies show that managers and consumers in the United States and the United Kingdom alike believe that good corporate citizenship is beneficial to company financial performance'[39]. Similarly, the Centre for Tomorrow's Company has concluded that despite measurement problems, there is strong evidence that successful companies in the 21st century will be rooted in a clearly defined set of values that guide and deepen key stakeholder relationships[40].

New Sources of Business Value

Disability can be understood in terms of the significance for business of values based on knowledge and trust in relationships between the company and key stakeholders. Several studies suggest that having a core set of values to which employees can relate can be the critical factor in business longevity. Hall, for example, found this to be true of over 90 per cent of a sample of 'long surviving' UK companies which started trading prior to 1880. For the majority, neither their senior management nor their staff saw profit as being their primary objective[41]. This is entirely consistent with the well-known US-based study, 'Built to Last', by Colins and Porras[42], which also concluded that companies which built a core set of values to guide their behaviour outperformed the stock market several times over.

Such intangibles have proved to be increasingly important throughout the twentieth century; they will be absolutely critical in the coming decades. As the Future Foundation points out in a report to BT, "a company's social capital - essentially durable trust-based relationships with their stakeholders - will increasingly determine competitive advantage and business success"[43]. This is reflected in the high and growing proportion of overall market value made up of intangible assets, which includes reputation with key stakeholders, and internal and network-based knowledge. One recent study by Interbrand, for example, concluded that a full one-quarter of global financial wealth is made up of brands as valued by the financial markets[44].

Globalisation accentuates the need to define common values as a basis for integrating organisations which are increasingly diverse in terms of geography, function and culture. There are few, if any, large companies - and fewer and fewer medium sized ones - which do not trade or produce internationally. These organisations must become more cosmopolitan in the broadest sense of embracing diversity, if they are to compete and navigate through their increasingly dynamic business environment.

FACTS

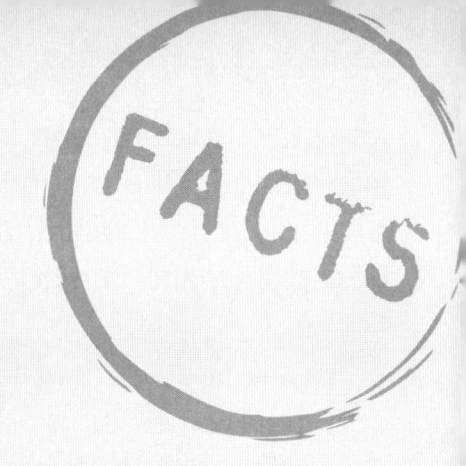

There are in the UK:

- **over 8.7 million disabled people**

- **two million disabled people in work**

- **a large and growing proportion of existing and potential customers, staff and shareholders who are conscious of disability through their personal situation and responsibilities (in the UK 6 million people describe themselves as carers)**

- **other stakeholder groups that experience discrimination and empathise**

- **those who are sensitised to such practical and human rights issues through their participation in an increasingly heterogeneous society**

In a 1996 study of the performance of the US retail company Sears in responding to the Americans with Disability Act (1990), the company's then Chair and CEO concluded 'at the bottom line, when Sears hires, works with, and accommodates qualified employees with disabilities, Sears enhances its customer base, employee morale, and its overall business strategy'[45].

In a climate where citizenship will increasingly drive business and government agendas, the increasing awareness of disability as a civil and human rights issue will also underpin a more inclusive and sophisticated corporate world view.

As business gains experience in employing disabled people; as business becomes aware of the numbers of disabled people already successfully employed and as organisations see the financial and business benefits that flow from anticipating the needs of all their customers, so the awareness of disability as a business priority grows.

Recent research by the DfEE gives a representative breakdown of occupations of disabled people in the UK.

Occupational characteristics of disabled employees compared to non-disabled

Occupation	%	Non
Managers and administrators	10	15
Professional occupations	10	10
Associate professionals	10	10
Clerical and secretarial	16	17
Craft and related	10	10
Personal and protective services	12	11
Sales occupations	7	9
Plant and machinery operatives	12	10
Other occupations	10	8
Not stated/insufficient information	2	–

Source:
Employment of Disabled People:
Assessing the Extent of Participation,
Research DfEE Research Report 69. 1999

This trend towards positioning disability as a business priority is accelerated by business-led initiatives such as the Employers' Forum on Disability in the UK which facilitates business to business communication and contact between employers and disabled individuals. The Forum has seen increased international interest in its method of operation.

Thus we can expect to see business leaders moving towards the routine inclusion of a disability dimension whenever they address the corporate and societal benefits that flow from:

- a genuinely diverse workforce and ethical employment practices

- quality people management systems to include excellence in developing people; in occupational health and promotion of a healthy workplace; in health and safety; in equal opportunities

- brand loyalty and distinctiveness associated with excellence in valuing all customers (and employees) as individuals

- enlightened corporate social responsibilities policies reflecting an accurate understanding of the communities and countries in which the organisation operates

- enabling the entire business to become disability confident

Business – Addressing the Disability dimension

The business
- **New economy globalisation diversity**
- **Human rights**
- **Marketing and communication**
- **IT and websites**
- **Product development and design**
- **Training and quality assurance**
- **Corporate social responsibility**
- **Human resources**
- **Customer care and market research**
- **Occupational health and health safety**
- **Property**
- **Press and PR**
- **New society government relations**
- **Legal**

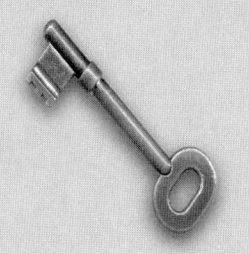

Diversity Futures 11

There is no shortage of futuristic scene setting. Two of the more interesting are those of the World Business Council for Sustainable Development (WBCSD)[46] and the Chatham House Forum under the Royal Institute for International Affairs (RIIA)[47]. Both offer positive and negative visions. Both point to social and environmental dislocation as being the principal outcomes of poor decisions now, and the subsequent cause of 'failed development' across society. Both point to the need for organisations to act now in creative and radical ways to avoid social and environmental 'bads' and realise the 'goods'.

These two studies assess business success in the context of increasingly heterogeneous societies. They highlight the increased choice pathways for consumers, employees, shareholders and other stakeholders, particularly in the light of changing technology. Both point to these choices being increasingly based on 'life style' and perceptions of values alignment - essentially a stakeholder's sense of social identity with branded options.

Explicit shared values, as well as people management systems which enable businesses to navigate through dynamic and highly diverse societies and markets, will be a key ingredient of success.

It is in this context that corporate social responsibility has emerged as a significant driver of corporate change. Ethics, human rights, and trust are but a few of the concepts around which leading businesses are increasingly organised.

Disability has been notably absent from many of the emerging debates and practices under the rubric of corporate social responsibility. One survey[48] confirmed that most intermediaries working in the field of corporate social responsibility simply assumed (without evidence) that disability was somehow automatically subsumed within the more general debate of 'inclusivity' and 'stakeholder accountability'[49]. It is only with the growing awareness that corporate social responsibility incorporates ethical employment practices that disability as a genuine and distinct priority is coming into focus.

As think-tanks like DEMOS and The Fabian Society begin to incorporate disability into their world view, so we can expect an increasing sophistication across the corporate social responsibility arena and an increasing awareness of disability as it affects every aspect of their analyses.

Disabled People in Tomorrow's Companies

Disabled people may be able to take advantage of new economic opportunities arising through technological and other changes. But for this to be realised, disabled people will be required to rapidly and continually evolve their own skill base.

Predicted shifts in workplace practices, emerging in the main from technological changes, need to be taken into account. These can be summarised as:

- companies being increasingly 'extended' over space and time

- associated shifts towards more flexible and specialised options for contributing to business, both in terms of place and time and timing of work. (For example a company in Dublin processing day-to-day invoices for an organisation in New York)

- rapidly evolving demands for skills, knowledge and lifelong learning[50]

These characteristics of the changing workplace could be regarded as good news. Disabled people will have increased opportunities to make contributions that build from their strengths and marginalise any relative individual impairments. There are, however, two potential problems.

The need for adaptability and rapid evolution of skills does not fit with the current relatively low level of education and professional competencies of the disabled community as compared to the overall population. Disabled people today are twice as likely as their non-disabled counterparts to have no formal qualifications[51].

In addition, the 'extensions' in business process in terms of time and space, including homeworking could further reduce that 'face-to-face' dialogue between non-disabled and disabled people which is needed to overcome prejudices reinforced by lack of personal experience and fear. The relatively low and falling level of socialisation of disabled people is already a noted and quantified phenomenon. A recent survey by the National Organisation on Disability in the USA concluded that 30 per cent of disabled people do not socialise with friends and family even once a week, a rise of almost 10 per cent since the mid-1980s[52].

These two challenges are arguably related. New skills development is, in part, acquired through formal training in the workplace or educational establishments. But increasingly, skill development needs will be identified and, in part, skills actually acquired informally, through social networks. One effect of technology could be to further isolate disabled people from, or 'specialise', their work related and social networks. If this is not overcome, disabled people may find themselves further marginalised from the workplace. This is akin to the problem identified by DEMOS of long term unemployed, who are further disadvantaged by the deep social networks of the unemployed which reinforce the status quo for all concerned[53].

Enabling Technology

Technology will enable many more disabled people to work than ever before. The Web, in particular, has the potential to offer disabled people unparalleled opportunities to interact and contribute their experiences, skills and purchasing power. Yet, for some reasons, many IT and new economy leaders have failed to understand these possibilities.

BT recently sponsored 'Accessible Website Design – a practical and strategic guide', published by the Employers' Forum on Disability. The guide, the first of its kind, positions a persuasive business case alongside the key technical issues of Web design and argues; 'Accessible Web design does not prevent organisations from using multimedia or presenting high quality design and production values. It simply enables organisations to think strategically about how to make it easy for everyone to interact with their Websites'.

Accessible Web Design also provides a strategic planning framework – the Website Agenda on Customers – making it easier for organisations to develop and share best practice, design action plans and measure progress. The Agenda signals a new way of thinking about Information Technology.

The Employers' Forum on Disability - The Website Agenda on Customers

Policy and top level commitment: Service to disabled customers will form an integral part of the company's product and service standards. A company-wide commitment to accessible Website design will be agreed by the top team and communicated to the rest of the company.

Market Research: As part of the Web design process, companies will specifically identify the needs of their disabled customers.

Design of products and services for all: Disabled people will be consulted on product and service design, both as experts and as consumers, whenever possible. Regular reviews of the accessibility to disabled people of products and services, including Websites, will be undertaken and acted upon.

Staff training and disability awareness: Specific steps will be taken to raise awareness of Web accessibility issues among employees involved in developing, marketing and delivering Web products and services to customers.

Communication with customers: The availability of accessible products and services, including Websites will be communicated to disabled customers. Advertising and other images will reflect a diverse customer base. A variety of formats will be used in your communications with customers.

Influencing other organisations: Major suppliers, contractors and franchises will be encouraged to have accessible Websites.

Involvement in the wider community: The company will recognise and respond to disabled people as suppliers, shareholders, employees and members of the community.

Monitoring performance: Progress in implementing the key points of this Agenda will be monitored at Executive level.

USA

- in 1999, Congress passed a law regarding accessibility and Websites. It currently requires any public Website to be made accessible to disabled Web users and there is growing pressure to expand this law to encompass commercial Websites

Australia

- since December 2000, all government departments are required to ensure their Websites are accessible

UK

- there is now a duty to make services accessible to people with disabilities and many people interpret this to include Websites. Legal requirements will be clarified as case law builds up. However, it would be prudent for organisations to take a best practice approach. As expectations of disabled customers rise, organisations can expect to be closely monitored on their performance in this area

IBM and Philips are to collaborate on the world-wide advancement of speech recognition technology[54]. Voice recognition systems, such as IBM's ViaVoice and Dragon system's DragonDictate, open opportunities for disabled users who are not able to use keyboards and other traditional input devices.

Also on the horizon is brain-body control technology[55], allowing interaction with a computer system by combining eye movement, facial muscle, and brain-wave bio-potentials to generate computer inputs. Eye tracking technology[56] will enable users to work a computer through eye movements alone.

Additionally, there is research on 'intelligent' buildings[57]. Anyone entering with a special smart card will trigger the building to adapt to the individual i.e. If the card user is visually impaired they can be spoken to by the computer system, through speakers around the building. Simple sound signals can be used to guide them from place to place.

Recommendations and Commitments 12

Business, alone, can not create the enabling environment required if significantly more disabled people are to contribute to tomorrow's company and to the economy. Building an enabling business environment in the future will require the combined forces of business, government and non-profit organisations. Much needs to be done by the many individuals and organisations committed to positive change.

THE FUTURE

GOVERNMENT NEEDS TO:

- focus on overcoming ignorance and fear of disabled people with a particular emphasis on the education of young people

- **build an enabling environment within its own institutions to improve its own ability to effectively understand and address the needs of business and disabled people**

- monitor the outcomes (not only compliance) of recent legislation, particularly the Disability Discrimination Act, for both disabled people and business

- be seen as a role model and exemplify the spirit of the legislation through its employment of, and service provisions to, disabled people

THE FUTURE

NON-PROFIT ORGANISATIONS NEED TO:

- develop their understanding of business needs and so enhance their capacity as intermediaries to support access for disabled people to work opportunities

- **establish, with business, an effective basis for building process and outcome performance measures which bring disabled people into existing and evolving social accountability and quality assurance standards**

- work with other stakeholders to enhance the leadership potential of disabled people as social and wealth creating entrepreneurs

THE FUTURE

BUSINESS NEEDS TO:

- deepen its ability to learn from and about disabled people and so strengthen its ability to access their talents and other contributions to business success

- **ensure that high-level business strategies explicitly set out to realise the potential of disabled people to contribute to business performance**

- engage in a systematic process of understanding and overcoming deeply-rooted prejudices and fears regarding disabled people within their organisations and society generally

THE FUTURE

COMMISSIONS WORLDWIDE NEED TO:

- address the 'digital divide'

- **bring about major shifts in awareness of, and attitudes to, disability**

- ensure dissemination of authoritative research data on, and examples of, successful practice in business and more widely

- **establish objective standards on good practice on employment and access**

- make it easier for employers and service providers to understand and meet their obligations under the law

employers' forum on disability

The Employer's Forum on Disability is committed to enabling people with impairments to contribute to, and gain from business success. Integral to its approach is the creation of alliances between disabled people, business, non-profit organisations and government that stimulate learning, engagement, and practical change. To this end, the Forum commits itself to:

- build capacity to enable member organisations to integrate disability strategically across their global business networks

- help business to overcome the stereotypes and the fears related to disability by linking representatives of business to disabled people and their organisations through innovative practical initiatives such as the new Leadership Programme spearheaded by organisations such as HSBC

- ensure the lead standards and audits which influence corporate social responsibility policies and behaviour appropriately address the disability dimension

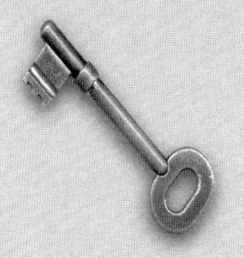

Conclusion 13

Successful organisations are those that monitor and meet shifts in societal expectations, control risks and anticipate market opportunities. These organisations, and their civil society and government equivalents, effectively mobilise the expertise and creative processes which enable them to take advantage of – and play an active role in – moulding the complex, dynamic world around them.

Disability is a part of this equation of success. Organisations that have the insight, will and know-how to engage with this growing part of the population will gain a competitive edge - through access to a growing spending power, a pool of skills and talents, and the support of disabled people as shareholders and stakeholders. These organisations will further benefit as the relatives, colleagues, friends and carers of disabled people respond in the marketplace to the way in which disabled people are treated by particular companies and by the business community as a whole.

Businesses that create an enabling environment for diverse parts of the community will prosper. For these companies, disabled people can and want to be a part of that equation of success. Such a pathway will also benefit society more generally, and so help to build a virtuous cycle that better balances social cohesion with economic competitiveness.

References

Chapter 2

1. The 8.7 million figure is for people with disabilities who could be covered by the DDA, it is a Department for Education and Employment (DfEE) estimate based on mid 1997 population estimates from the Office for National Statistics (ONS) and "Disability Discrimination Act: Analysis of Data from an Omnibus Survey", DSS In-house Report 30, July 1997. ISBN 1 85197 831 3

2. Enduring Economic Exclusion; Disabled People, Income and Work. Tania Burchardt, Joseph Rowntree Foundation, October 2000

3. Institute of Employment Studies research based on analysis of data from the DfEE disability survey (nationally representative sample of over 2000 disabled people: Meager et al: Employment of Disabled People: Assessing the Extent of Participation, DfEE Research Report, RR69, 1998

4. Makrotest (1998) Information and Communications technology for the Elderly and People with Disabilities, prepared for the Department of Trade and Industry, Makrotest, Tunbridge Wells

5. ibid

6. Enduring Economic Exclusion; Disabled People, Income and Work. Tania Burchardt, Joseph Rowntree Foundation, October 2000

7. National Institute of Disability Management and Research (1999) Making a Difference in the Workplace

8. Department of Social Security (1999) Government Expenditure Plans 1999-2000, DSS, London: Part 4: 85

9. ibid. 87

10. Margaret Hodge MP, Minister for Employment and Equal Opportunities

Chapter 3

11. Disability Discrimination Act 1995, HMSO, London , ISBN 0105450952

12. 1998 N.O.D./Harris Survey of Americans with Disabilities, NOD, Washington DC

13. Census Bureau's Survey of Income Program and Participation (SIPP), USA,1994

Chapter 5

14. J. Morrell (1990) The Employment of People with Disabilities, IFF Research Ltd, London

15. Sheena Stockdale, Equal Opportunities Manager, Marks and Spencer

16. National Institute of Disability Management & Research (1999)

17. DuPont (1991) Equal to the Task II: 1990 DuPont Survey of Employment of People with Disabilities, DuPont, Wilmington www.dupont.com/corp/people/disabled/extraord.html

18. Disability Management Program Graduates Making a Difference in the Workplace by Norman C. Hursh, ScD February 1997 - 8.5 x 11 - 23 pp - References ISBN 0-9682480-1-2

Chapter 6

19. Institute of Employment Studies, Estimating the spending power of disabled people, research commissioned by the Employers' Forum on Disability 1999.

20. The Grey Market in the UK 1994, executive summary, Key Note Ltd, http://www.keynote.co.uk/html/grey/grey01.html

21. Mike Freeney, Disability Matters Limited

22. N. Meager, C. Evans, N. Tackey and M. Williams (1998) Baseline Survey of the Measures in Part III of the Disability Discrimination Act 1995 Relating to the Provision of Goods and Services I, prepared by the Institute of Development Studies for the DfEE, DfEE, Sudbury

23. Tourism 2000, Tourism for all in Europe, Deloitte Touche 1993

24. Addleshaw Booth & Co, April 2000

25. The Grass Roots Group Plc (1998) The Challenge of Disability, The Grass Roots Group Plc, London

26. BT (1998) Putting Disability on the Agenda, BT, London: 93

27. EOR No. 81 September/October 1998: 20

Chapter 7

28. West et al (1998) Impact of People Management Practices on Business Performance, Institute of Personnel Management, London

29. Bilmes, L. (1998, forthcoming), Enlightened Employment.

30. RSA Inquiry (1995) Tomorrow's Company: the role of business in a changing world RSA. London.

31. Hutton, P. (1997) 'Using Research to Improve Quality and Service Provision'. Paper at SMI Conference on Measuring Service Provision, MORI, London.

32. Hutton, P. (1998) Customer Satisfaction - What Difference Does it Make?, MORI, London.

33. Integrating Disabled Employees: Case studies of 40 Employees. DfEE Research Report RR56. By Watson, A et al. DfEE (1998), ISBN 085522 732 X

Chapter 9

34. Schneider-Ross (1998) The Language of Equal Opportunities: Researching Line Managers' Reactions, unpublished research report, Employers' Forum on Disability, London

35. I. Lawson (1999) Leaders for Tomorrow's Society, The Industrial Society, London: 1

36. Louis Harris and Associates (1991) Public Attitudes Towards People with Disabilities, undertaken for National Organisation on Disability, Louis Harris and Associates, New York

37. Access Denied: Disabled people's experience of social exclusion. NOP Research Group. Leonard Cheshire 1998

38. J. Humphries and J. Rubery (1995) The Economics of Equal Opportunities, Equal Opportunities Commission, Manchester

Chapter 10

39. The Conference Board Europe (1999) The Link Between Corporate Citizenship and Financial Performance, The Conference Board Europe, Brussels

40. Centre for Tomorrow's Company (1998) The Inclusive Approach and Business Success, CTC, London

41. Hall, R. (1997) 'Long Term Survivors', Journal of General Management Vol. 22 No 4 Summer 1997

42. Colins, J. C. and Porras, J. L. (1995) Built to Last: Successful Habits of Visionary Companies, Random House, London.

43. Grimshaw, C. Howard, M. & Willmott, M. (1998) The Responsible Organisation: The Roles and Responsibilities of the Big Citizens of the 21st Century report commissioned by BT. London

44. Clifton, R. and E. Maughan (1999) The Future of Brands: Twenty Five Visions, MacMillan Business, London

45. P. Blanck (1997) Communicating the Americans with Disabilities Act: Transcending Compliance: 1996 Follow-Up Report on Sears, Roebuck and Co, Northwestern University, Washington

Chapter 11

46. WBCSD (1998) Exploring Sustainable Development: WBCSD Global Scenarios 2000-2050, WBCSD, Geneva

47. RIIA (1998) Navigating Uncharted Waters: Constructive Approaches to Complexity, RIIA, London

48. Undertaken for the National Disability Council

49. KPMG (1998) Corporate Social Responsibility. Is Disability a Priority ?? A Survey, prepared for the National Disability Council, KPMG, London

50. An Inclusive Future? Disability, Social Change, and Potential Opportunities for Greater Inclusion by 2010, I Christie and G Mensah-Coker DEMOS 1999.

51. DfEE Disability Briefing: November 1998

52. National Organisation on Disability (1998)

53. An Inclusive Future? Disability, Social Change, and Potential Opportunities for Greater Inclusion by 2010, I Christie and G Mensah-Coker DEMOS 1999.

54. Ability , IBM and Philips in collaboration deal, p 9, Issue 29 Summer 1999, VNU Business Publications

55. Ability, The missing link, p 12-13 Issue 29, Summer 1999, VNU Business Publications

56. Ability, Hands free, p 9, Issue 27, Winter 1998, VNU Business Publications

57. Ability, Chips in everything, p 12-13, Issue 28, Spring 1999, VNU Business Publications

Susan Scott Parker OBE

Susan Scott-Parker is the founding Chief Executive of the Employers' Forum on Disability. Established in 1986, the Forum is the first employers' organisation in the European Community working to make it easier to employ disabled people and serve disabled customers. The Forum has 375 members employing over 20 per cent of the UK workforce.

Susan is an acknowledged authority and commentator on the business advantages of embracing diversity and equal opportunities. She has considerable experience in assisting business to develop inter-sector partnerships, as well as to design complex change and communication programmes.

She is a member of the CBI Equal Opportunities Specialist Forum. She has also served as UNICE's disability expert to the European Disability Forum (Brussels), as a member of the Disability Rights Task Force and the National Disability Council.

Susan has worked as a consultant to central and local government, to the Kings Fund Centre and national voluntary organisations. As a Coverdale associate, she helped establish the first leadership bursary programme for disabled people.

Her publications include 'Disability Etiquette'; 'Media Disability Etiquette'; 'Monitoring People with Disabilities in the Workforce'; 'Welcoming Disabled Customers'; 'The Action File on Disability' and 'They Aren't in the Brief: Disabled People in Charity Advertising'.

Before arriving in the UK from Canada in 1981,

Susan advised disabled people on how to establish and market their own services and organisations, and worked with the government of Alberta. She published Canada's first market research into employers' responses to campaigns promoting job seekers with disabilities.

Simon Zadek

Dr Simon Zadek is Chair of the international professional body for social auditing, the Institute of Social and Ethical AccountAbility, having been Development Director of the New Economics Foundation and Chair of the Ethical Trading Initiative until the end of 1998. He is on the Steering Committee of the Global Reporting Initiative, the Operating Council of the Global Alliance for Workers and Communities, and the International Advisory Committee of the Copenhagen Centre.

Simon has contributed to the development and practice of corporate responsibility and accountability as a practitioner advisor and external verifier, in building multi-stakeholder alliances to promote good practice, and through his writing. He has co-edited several books, including Building Corporate AccountAbility (with Peter Pruzan and Richard Evans), and more recently Mediating Sustainability: Growing Policy from the Grass Roots (with Jutta Blauert). He has written on diverse topics such as environment and trade, indicators for sustainable development, Buddhist economics, social entrepreneurs, utopia and economics, ethical trade, civil regulation, new social partnerships, disability, and sustainable consumption.